PictoBlox Mastery: Advanced AI, Robotics, and Automation for Experts

A Professional Guide to AI, Automation, and Robotics Using PictoBlox

Introduction

Welcome to *PictoBlox Mastery*. This book is designed to take your understanding of PictoBlox beyond the basics, diving deep into advanced artificial intelligence (AI), automation, and robotics applications. Whether you are an educator, a professional, or a researcher, this guide will equip you with the knowledge and hands-on experience needed to build sophisticated projects using PictoBlox.

What Makes This an Advanced Guide?

Unlike beginner-level books that introduce you to the fundamentals of PictoBlox, this guide focuses on:

- **Complex AI Implementations** – Working with machine learning models, deep learning concepts, and computer vision.
- **Advanced Robotics & Automation** – Exploring sensor integration, autonomous decision-making, and IoT-based control systems.
- **Real-World Applications** – Implementing AI-driven solutions in education, industrial automation, and research.
- **Custom Extensions & Enhancements** – Expanding PictoBlox functionalities using Python, custom scripts, and external integrations.

By the end of this book, you will not only master PictoBlox's AI and robotics features but also develop real-world projects that push the boundaries of what's possible with block-based and text-based coding.

Who Is This Book For?

This book is designed for:

- **Educators** – Teachers and instructors looking to integrate advanced AI and robotics concepts into their curriculum.
- **Professionals** – Engineers, developers, and tech enthusiasts who want to prototype AI-powered automation systems.
- **Researchers** – Individuals working in AI, machine learning, and robotics who seek a user-friendly platform for experimentation and innovation.

While prior experience with PictoBlox or basic programming is recommended, this book will provide step-by-step guidance to help you navigate more complex topics.

How to Get the Most Out of This Book

To maximize your learning, follow these strategies:

1. **Hands-on Practice** – Engage with every project, experiment with modifications, and try implementing your own ideas.
2. **Use the Provided Resources** – Download code snippets, datasets, and supplementary materials referenced in the book.

3. **Leverage Online Communities** – Participate in PictoBlox forums, AI & robotics discussion groups, and open-source collaboration projects.
4. **Think Beyond the Book** – Apply the skills learned here to develop innovative solutions for real-world problems.

Chapter 1: Advanced AI and Machine Learning in PictoBlox

Artificial Intelligence (AI) and Machine Learning (ML) are transforming the way we interact with technology. From recognizing faces in security systems to automating conversations with chatbots, AI allows computers to analyze data, make decisions, and learn over time.

PictoBlox offers a powerful, block-based approach to implementing AI, making it easier to train and deploy machine learning models. In this chapter, we will explore how to:

- Train custom AI models with PictoBlox
- Use TensorFlow to enhance AI capabilities
- Develop face and object recognition systems for security applications
- Create AI-powered chatbots for interactive conversations

By the end of this chapter, you'll have the knowledge to build **real-world AI projects** using PictoBlox.

Training Custom AI Models

AI models are trained using **datasets**—collections of images, text, or numbers that the AI learns from. PictoBlox simplifies AI model training through tools like **Teachable Machine** and its built-in **Machine Learning (ML) Environment**.

Steps to Train a Custom AI Model in PictoBlox

1. **Collect and Label Data** – Gather images, sounds, or gestures relevant to your project.
2. **Train the Model** – Use PictoBlox's ML tools to help the AI recognize patterns.
3. **Test and Improve** – Evaluate accuracy, tweak the dataset, and retrain if needed.
4. **Deploy in PictoBlox** – Integrate the model into a project to make real-time predictions.

Example: AI-Based Image Classifier

Imagine you want to train an AI model to **classify different types of fruit**—apples, bananas, and oranges.

- Collect 50–100 images of each fruit.
- Upload them to PictoBlox's Machine Learning Environment.
- Train the AI model to recognize them.
- Use the trained model to classify new images in real-time.

Where can you use this?

- **Smart Farming:** Automatically sort fruits in a processing unit.
- **Retail Automation:** Help customers identify produce in self-checkout machines.
- **Educational Projects:** Teach AI concepts to students in a fun way.

Using TensorFlow with PictoBlox

TensorFlow is one of the most widely used AI frameworks. While PictoBlox has built-in AI tools, TensorFlow allows you to:

- **Train more complex AI models**
- **Use pre-trained models** (such as handwriting recognition or image classification)
- **Optimize AI performance for speed and accuracy**

Example: AI-Powered Handwriting Recognition

Let's say you want to build a system that recognizes handwritten digits (0-9).

1. **Use the MNIST dataset** – A well-known dataset of 70,000 handwritten digits.

2. **Train a model using TensorFlow** – Convert images into numerical data for AI to recognize patterns.
3. **Deploy the trained model in PictoBlox** – Use it to read handwritten input and convert it into text.

Where can you use this?

- **Smart Notepads:** Convert handwritten notes into digital text.
- **Math Learning Apps:** Help students practice and get real-time feedback.
- **Automated Banking Systems:** Recognize handwritten checks or forms.

Face and Object Recognition for Security Systems

AI-driven security systems use **computer vision** to detect and identify faces, objects, or intrusions. PictoBlox provides **face recognition** and **object detection** tools that allow you to:

- Detect human faces and match them to a database.
- Identify objects (e.g., detecting a suspicious package in a public area).

- Trigger automated security alerts when an unknown face or object is detected.

Example: AI-Based Intruder Alert System

Imagine you want to create a security system for your home that **detects unauthorized persons**.

1. **Train the AI model** with images of authorized family members.
2. **Set up a camera** connected to PictoBlox.
3. **Program an alert system** – If an unrecognized person enters, trigger an alarm.
4. **Integrate IoT for remote monitoring** – Send alerts to your phone via the internet.

Where can you use this?

- **Smart Homes:** Prevent unauthorized entry.
- **Office Security:** Allow only registered employees.
- **Public Surveillance:** Detect persons of interest in high-security zones.

Creating AI-Based Chatbots

AI chatbots are **virtual assistants** that understand and respond to human conversations. PictoBlox allows you to build chatbots using:

- **Text-based AI models** to understand user inputs.
- **Natural Language Processing (NLP)** to improve chatbot responses.
- **Speech-to-text & text-to-speech** for voice interaction.

Hands-On Project: AI-Powered Virtual Assistant

Project Goal

Create an **AI chatbot** in PictoBlox that can answer questions, tell jokes, and give useful information.

What You'll Need

- PictoBlox installed on your computer.
- Internet access for chatbot integration.
- A microphone (optional, for voice interaction).

Step 1: Set Up the Chatbot in PictoBlox

1. **Open PictoBlox** and create a new project.
2. **Go to the Extensions menu** and add the **Artificial Intelligence** and **Text Recognition** extensions.
3. **Create a new sprite** for your chatbot character (e.g., a talking robot).

Step 2: Code the Chatbot Responses

1. Use the **"Ask and wait"** block to collect user input.
2. Use **if-else** conditions to respond appropriately:

scratch

```
when green flag clicked
say "Hello! Ask me anything!"
forever
    ask "What do you want to know?" and wait
    if (answer contains "weather") then
        say "Today's weather is sunny with a high of 25°C."
    else if (answer contains "joke") then
        say "Why don't scientists trust atoms? Because they make up everything!"
    else
```

say "I'm still learning! Try asking something else."

Step 3: Add Speech Interaction (Optional)

1. Add the **Text-to-Speech** extension in PictoBlox.
2. Modify your script to make the chatbot talk:

scratch

```
when green flag clicked
say "Hello! I can talk now!"
forever
    ask "What do you want to know?" and wait
    if (answer contains "weather") then
        speak "Today's weather is sunny with a high of 25 degrees."
    else if (answer contains "joke") then
        speak "Why don't scientists trust atoms? Because they make up everything!"
    else
        speak "I'm still learning! Try asking something else."
```

Step 4: Test and Improve

- Add **more questions** and answers to make your chatbot smarter.

- Integrate **speech-to-text** so users can talk instead of typing.
- Use **external APIs** (like OpenAI or Google) for advanced responses.

Final Thoughts

In this chapter, you learned:
- How to train custom AI models for PictoBlox.
- How to integrate TensorFlow for advanced AI applications.
- How to build AI-powered security systems.
- How to create interactive AI chatbots.

Next, we'll dive into **Advanced Robotics and Automation**, where we'll explore how to control robots, automate tasks, and create self-learning machines.

Chapter 2: Internet of Things (IoT) with PictoBlox

Introduction to IoT and Cloud Integration

The **Internet of Things (IoT)** connects physical devices to the internet, allowing them to **collect, exchange, and analyze data**. From smart homes to industrial automation, IoT is revolutionizing modern technology.

Why Use PictoBlox for IoT?

- **User-Friendly** – No complex coding required, making IoT accessible to beginners and experts alike.
- **Cloud Integration** – Connect with **Google Sheets, Firebase, and other IoT platforms** to store and analyze data.
- **Automation & Control** – Remotely control devices like **lights, fans, and sensors** from anywhere in the world.
- **Real-Time Monitoring** – Track temperature, humidity, motion, and other sensor data remotely.

Connecting PictoBlox with Firebase and Google Sheets

Why Firebase and Google Sheets?

- **Google Sheets** – Stores IoT data in real-time for tracking and analysis.
- **Firebase** – A powerful cloud database that allows real-time device control and data synchronization.

Setting Up Firebase for IoT in PictoBlox

Step 1: Create a Firebase Project

1. Go to **Firebase Console** and create a new project.
2. Add a **Realtime Database** and set it to **public** or configure authentication.
3. Copy the **Database URL**—you'll need it to connect PictoBlox to Firebase.

Step 2: Set Up PictoBlox to Send Data to Firebase

1. Open PictoBlox and add the **IoT Extension**.
2. Connect your Wi-Fi-enabled board (e.g., **ESP8266 or ESP32**) to PictoBlox.
3. Use the following blocks to send sensor data to Firebase:

scratch

when green flag clicked
set Wi-Fi SSID to "your_WiFi_name" and password to "your_WiFi_password"
connect to Firebase at "your_firebase_database_url"
forever
   read temperature from D1
   upload data to Firebase at "/home/temperature" value (temperature)
   wait 10 seconds

Example: Storing Temperature and Humidity Data in Google Sheets

Step 1: Set Up Google Sheets Integration

1. Create a Google Sheet and open **App Script** (Extensions > Apps Script).
2. Add this script to allow IoT devices to send data:

javascript

```javascript
function doPost(e) {
    var sheet = SpreadsheetApp.getActiveSpreadsheet().getActiveSheet();
    var data = JSON.parse(e.postData.contents);
```

```
sheet.appendRow([new            Date(),
data.temperature, data.humidity]);
    return
ContentService.createTextOutput("Success
");
}
```

3. Publish the script as a **web app** and copy the URL.

Step 2: Send Data from PictoBlox to Google Sheets

Modify your PictoBlox script:

scratch

```
when green flag clicked
set Wi-Fi SSID to "your_WiFi_name" and
password to "your_WiFi_password"
connect to Web API "your_google_script_url"
forever
    read temperature from D1
    read humidity from D2
    send data to Web API {"temperature":
temperature, "humidity": humidity}
    wait 10 seconds
```

Home Automation: Controlling Devices Over the Internet

Home automation allows you to remotely control **lights, fans, door locks, and appliances** via the internet.

Example: Controlling a Light Bulb from a Mobile App

What You Need

- **ESP8266 or ESP32** microcontroller
- **Relay module** to switch the light on/off
- **Firebase** as the cloud server

Step 1: Update Firebase with Light Status

Use this Firebase block in PictoBlox:

scratch

```
when green flag clicked
set Wi-Fi SSID to "your_WiFi_name" and
password to "your_WiFi_password"
connect          to          Firebase          at
"your_firebase_database_url"
forever
   if (Firebase value at "/home/light") = 1
   then turn on relay at D3
   else turn off relay at D3
   wait 2 seconds
```

Step 2: Create a Web-Based Switch

Use an **HTML button** connected to Firebase:

html

```
<button            onclick="toggleLight(1)">Turn
ON</button>
<button            onclick="toggleLight(0)">Turn
OFF</button>

<script>
function toggleLight(state) {
    fetch('your_firebase_database_url/home.json',
{
      method: 'PUT',
      body: JSON.stringify({ light: state })
    });
}
</script>
```

- Now you can **control your light from a web app**
from anywhere in the world!

Data Logging and Remote Monitoring

Remote monitoring allows users to track data like
temperature, humidity, motion, or air quality
in real-time.

Example: Air Quality Monitoring System

What You Need

- **MQ-135 Air Quality Sensor**
- **ESP8266 or ESP32**
- **Firebase or Google Sheets**

Step 1: Read Air Quality Data

1. Connect the MQ-135 sensor to **A0** on your microcontroller.
2. Write this PictoBlox script:

scratch

when green flag clicked
set Wi-Fi SSID to "your_WiFi_name" and password to "your_WiFi_password"
connect to Firebase at "your_firebase_database_url"
forever
   read air quality from A0
   upload data to Firebase at "/home/air_quality" value (air quality)
   wait 5 seconds

Step 2: Display the Data on a Mobile Dashboard

1. Use **Google Sheets** or **Blynk App** to visualize air quality in real time.

2. Set alerts when air quality reaches dangerous levels.

- **Applications**: Smart cities, industrial monitoring, personal air quality tracking.

Hands-On Project: IoT-Based Smart Weather Station

Project Goal

Create an **IoT-based smart weather station** that monitors **temperature, humidity, and light intensity**, storing data in **Google Sheets** and displaying it in **real time** on a mobile-friendly dashboard.

What You'll Need

- **ESP8266 or ESP32**
- **DHT11 sensor (temperature & humidity)**
- **LDR sensor (light intensity)**
- **Google Sheets for data storage**

Step 1: Connect Sensors

1. **DHT11** – Connect **VCC to 3.3V, GND to GND, and Data to D2**.

2. **LDR Sensor** – Connect **one leg to A0 and the other to 3.3V with a pull-down resistor**.

Step 2: Send Data to Google Sheets

Modify your PictoBlox script:

scratch

when green flag clicked
set Wi-Fi SSID to "your_WiFi_name" and password to "your_WiFi_password"
connect to Web API "your_google_script_url"
forever
   read temperature from D2
   read humidity from D3
   read light intensity from A0
   send data to Web API {"temperature": temperature, "humidity": humidity, "light": light_intensity}
   wait 10 seconds

Step 3: Create a Mobile Dashboard

Use **Google Sheets charts** or **Blynk App** to visualize real-time weather data on your phone.

- **Congratulations!** You've built a **real-time weather station** that logs data in the cloud and can be accessed from anywhere!

Final Thoughts

In this chapter, you learned:
- How to connect PictoBlox to **Firebase and Google Sheets**.
- How to build **home automation** systems with IoT.
- How to create **remote monitoring** solutions using cloud databases.
- How to build an **IoT-based smart weather station**.

Chapter 3: Advanced Robotics with PictoBlox

Robotics and AI are revolutionizing industries, from **automation and healthcare to space exploration and defense**. PictoBlox allows you to **design, program, and control advanced robots** with AI-powered features such as **gesture recognition, obstacle avoidance, and swarm coordination**.

Why Use PictoBlox for Advanced Robotics?

- **AI Integration** – Train and use **custom AI models** for autonomous robots.
- **IoT Compatibility** – Control and monitor robots remotely.
- **Hardware Support** – Works with **Arduino, ESP32, micro:bit, and TinkerGen's robotic kits**.
- **Visual Programming & Python** – Transition from block-based coding to Python for complex logic.

Using AI for Autonomous Robotics

Autonomous robots use **sensors, AI, and control algorithms** to navigate and interact with the environment **without human intervention**.

Example: AI-Powered Line-Following Robot

What You Need

- **PictoBlox with AI & Robotics Extensions**
- **Arduino Uno + Motor Driver (L298N) + IR Sensors**
- **AI Model (Optional for Traffic Sign Recognition)**

Step 1: Assemble the Robot

1. **IR Sensors** – Place **two IR sensors** under the robot to detect the black line.
2. **Motors** – Connect **DC motors to the L298N driver** for movement.

Step 2: Program the Line-Following Algorithm

scratch

```
when green flag clicked
forever
   if (left sensor = black and right sensor = white) then
      turn left
   else if (left sensor = white and right sensor = black) then
      turn right
   else
      move forward
   wait 0.1 seconds
```

- Now, the robot follows a **black track** on a white surface!

Step 3: AI-Powered Sign Recognition (Optional)

- Train an AI model in **PictoBlox** to recognize **STOP, LEFT, RIGHT** signs.
- Modify the robot's behavior based on sign detection:

scratch

when AI detects "STOP" sign
stop motors
wait 5 seconds
resume movement

- This allows your robot to **respond to traffic signs** like a self-driving car!

Gesture-Controlled Robots

Gesture control enables **hands-free** robot operation using **camera-based AI or accelerometers** (like in micro:bit or MPU6050).

Example: Hand Gesture Robot Using PictoBlox AI

What You Need

- **Webcam or micro:bit accelerometer**
- **PictoBlox AI Extension**
- **Arduino with Motor Driver**

Step 1: Train AI for Hand Gestures

1. Open **PictoBlox** → AI Extension → **Pose Classifier**.
2. Capture **four gestures** (UP, DOWN, LEFT, RIGHT).
3. Train the model and deploy it in PictoBlox.

Step 2: Control the Robot with AI

scratch

when green flag clicked
forever
    if (AI detects "UP" gesture) then move forward
    if (AI detects "DOWN" gesture) then move backward
    if (AI detects "LEFT" gesture) then turn left
    if (AI detects "RIGHT" gesture) then turn right

- Now, you can **control the robot using hand movements**!

Swarm Robotics: Coordinating Multiple Bots

Swarm robotics enables **multiple robots to work together**, inspired by **bee colonies and ant behavior**.

Example: Coordinating Two Robots Using Bluetooth

What You Need

- **Two micro:bit controllers** (or ESP32 with Wi-Fi)
- **PictoBlox Bluetooth Extension**

Step 1: Assign Leader and Follower

- **Leader Robot** sends movement commands.
- **Follower Robot** replicates movements **using Bluetooth/Wi-Fi**.

Step 2: Write the Leader Robot Code

scratch

```
when green flag clicked
forever
    if (button A pressed) then send "forward" via
Bluetooth
    if (button B pressed) then send "left" via
Bluetooth
```

Step 3: Write the Follower Robot Code

scratch

when green flag clicked
forever
    if (received "forward") then move forward
    if (received "left") then turn left

- Now, the **second robot follows the leader**, useful in warehouse automation and military applications.

AI-Based Obstacle Avoidance

Obstacle avoidance is essential for **autonomous navigation** in drones, self-driving cars, and delivery robots.

Example: AI-Based Obstacle Avoidance Using Ultrasonic Sensors

What You Need

- **Arduino + Ultrasonic Sensor (HC-SR04)**
- **Motor Driver for Movement**

Step 1: Read Distance Data

scratch

when green flag clicked

forever

    set distance = read ultrasonic sensor from D2

Step 2: Avoid Obstacles with AI Decision Making

scratch

forever

    if (distance < 20 cm) then

        stop motors

        turn right for 1 second

    else

        move forward

- Now, the robot **detects obstacles and changes direction** to avoid collisions!

Hands-On Project: AI-Powered Patrol Robot

Project Goal

Build an **AI-powered patrol robot** that:
- **Patrols an area** using a pre-defined path.
- **Detects intruders** using AI and **face recognition**.
- **Alerts the user via IoT (Firebase or Blynk)**.

Step 1: Assemble the Robot

- **ESP32/Arduino + Camera Module** (for face recognition).
- **Ultrasonic Sensors** (for obstacle avoidance).
- **Wi-Fi Module (ESP32)** (for cloud alerts).

Step 2: Train AI for Face Recognition

1. Open **PictoBlox AI Extension → Face Detection**.
2. Train it to recognize "Owner" and "Unknown".
3. If an unknown face is detected, send an alert.

Step 3: Patrol Movement & AI-Based Detection

scratch

when green flag clicked
forever
    move forward

```
if (AI detects "Unknown" face) then
    stop motors
    send alert to Firebase "Intruder detected!"
    take picture and upload
```

Step 4: Send Alerts to a Mobile App (Using Firebase)

scratch

```
when AI detects "Unknown" face
    upload image to Firebase
    send notification "Intruder detected!" to mobile
```

- **Your patrol robot now detects intruders and sends real-time alerts!**

Final Thoughts

In this chapter, you learned:
- How to build an **AI-powered line-following robot**.
- How to create a **gesture-controlled robot**.
- How to implement **swarm robotics** for group coordination.
- How to use **AI for obstacle avoidance and security patrol**.

Chapter 4: Advanced Sensors and Actuators

Advanced sensors and actuators **bridge the gap between AI, automation, and robotics**, allowing systems to perceive and interact with their environments. This chapter explores **LiDAR, ultrasonic, GPS, and environmental sensors**, demonstrating how AI can enhance decision-making for **real-world automation**.

Why Are Advanced Sensors Important?

- **Precision** – LiDAR and GPS improve navigation accuracy.
- **Real-time Data** – Environmental sensors help in **weather monitoring, agriculture, and smart homes**.
- **AI Integration** – AI-powered decision-making enhances automation efficiency.

Using LiDAR, Ultrasonic, and GPS Sensors

1□ LiDAR for Obstacle Detection and Mapping

LiDAR (Light Detection and Ranging) uses **laser pulses** to measure distances and create **3D maps** of the surroundings.

Example: AI-Powered LiDAR Obstacle Avoidance

Use case: Self-driving cars, drones, warehouse robots.

What You Need:

- **TFmini-S LiDAR Sensor** (or RPLIDAR for full 360° mapping)
- **Arduino or ESP32**
- **PictoBlox AI Extension**

Code Snippet (Detecting Obstacles with LiDAR)

scratch

```
when green flag clicked
forever
    set distance = read LiDAR sensor
    if (distance < 30 cm) then
        stop motors
        turn right
```

- Now, the robot **detects obstacles and avoids collisions using LiDAR!**

2️⃣ Ultrasonic Sensors for Short-Range Detection

Ultrasonic sensors work like LiDAR but use **sound waves** instead of lasers.

Example: AI-Based Object Sorting System

Use case: Smart waste segregation, conveyor belt automation.

What You Need:

- **Ultrasonic Sensor (HC-SR04)**
- **Servo Motor** (for sorting mechanism)
- **PictoBlox AI Model (Object Recognition)**

Code Snippet (Detecting Object Size & Sorting)

scratch

```
when object detected
    set distance = ultrasonic sensor reading
    if (distance < 5 cm) then
        move object to "Small bin"
    else
        move object to "Large bin"
```

- The system **automatically sorts objects based on size!**

3️ GPS for Autonomous Navigation

GPS helps robots, drones, and vehicles navigate large areas **outdoors**.

Example: GPS-Guided Delivery Robot

Use case: Last-mile delivery, autonomous farming, drone navigation.

What You Need:

- **Neo-6M GPS Module**
- **ESP32 or Raspberry Pi**
- **PictoBlox IoT & AI Extensions**

Code Snippet (Navigating to a Predefined Location)

scratch

```
when green flag clicked
forever
   set current_location = read GPS data
   if (current_location ≠ target_location) then
      move towards target
   else
      stop motors
      send "Arrived at destination" alert
```

- The robot **automatically reaches a GPS-defined target location!**

Smart Automation with Environmental Sensors

Environmental sensors **detect temperature, humidity, air quality, and light levels** for smart applications.

1️⃣AI-Based Weather Station

Use case: Smart farming, air pollution monitoring, climate studies.

What You Need:

- **DHT11 Sensor (Temperature & Humidity)**
- **BMP180 (Pressure & Altitude)**
- **ESP32 for IoT Connectivity**

Code Snippet (AI Predicting Weather Conditions)

scratch

```
when green flag clicked
forever
    read temperature, humidity, pressure
    send data to AI model
    if (AI predicts "Rain") then
        display "Carry an umbrella!"
```

- The system **predicts weather patterns using AI!**

2️⃣ Smart Indoor Lighting with AI & Motion Sensors

Use case: Home automation, energy efficiency.

What You Need:

- **PIR Motion Sensor**
- **LDR (Light Sensor)**
- **Relay Module (To Control Lights)**

Code Snippet (AI-Based Smart Lighting System)

scratch

```
when motion detected
    if (light level < 50%) then
        turn ON lights
    else
        keep lights OFF
```

- Lights **automatically turn on only when needed**, saving energy!

Integrating AI with Hardware for Decision Making

AI can process sensor data in **real-time**, making smart decisions without human intervention.

Example: AI-Powered Fire Detection & Alarm System

Use case: Smart buildings, industrial safety.

What You Need:

- **MQ-2 Gas Sensor (for smoke detection)**
- **Thermal Camera or IR Sensor**
- **AI Model for Image Recognition**

Code Snippet (AI Identifying Fire & Triggering Alarm)

scratch

```
when fire detected by AI
    activate alarm
    send alert to mobile
    if (AI confirms fire for 5 seconds) then
        activate sprinkler system
```

- The system **detects fire, triggers an alarm, and activates sprinklers automatically**!

Hands-On Project: AI-Powered Smart Greenhouse

Project Goal

- Monitor and control temperature, humidity, and soil moisture.
- Use AI to detect plant health.
- Automate watering and ventilation.

Step 1: Collect Sensor Data

- **DHT11** – Measures **temperature & humidity**.
- **Soil Moisture Sensor** – Checks if plants need water.
- **Light Sensor** – Monitors sunlight levels.

scratch

```
when green flag clicked
forever
    set temperature = read DHT11
    set soil_moisture = read soil sensor
```

Step 2: AI-Based Decision Making

- Train an AI model in **PictoBlox** to recognize **healthy vs unhealthy plants**.
- AI decides **when to water and ventilate the greenhouse**.

scratch

when AI detects "unhealthy plant"
    if (soil moisture < 30%) then
        turn ON water pump
    else
        increase ventilation

- The greenhouse **automatically optimizes conditions for healthy plant growth**!

Final Thoughts

In this chapter, you learned:
- How to use **LiDAR, ultrasonic, and GPS** for navigation.
- How **environmental sensors** enable smart automation.
- How **AI improves decision-making** in hardware systems.

Chapter 5: Creating AI-Powered Games and Interactive Applications

AI is transforming gaming and interactive applications by enabling **dynamic gameplay, speech interactions, and smart visual processing**. In this chapter, you'll learn how to **develop AI-powered games in PictoBlox** using:

- **Machine Learning for Adaptive Gameplay**
- **Speech Recognition for Voice-Controlled Games**
- **AI-Based Image Processing for Game Mechanics**

By the end, you'll build a **hands-on AI-powered interactive game!**

Game Development with AI in PictoBlox

AI can **enhance game mechanics** by allowing characters to learn, respond to player behavior, and adapt strategies.

Example 1: AI-Powered Adaptive Enemy

Use case: AI-controlled enemies that get smarter as the player progresses.

How It Works:

- The AI **tracks the player's moves** and **adjusts enemy difficulty** dynamically.
- If the player **wins multiple times**, the enemy **increases speed or changes tactics**.

What You Need:

- **PictoBlox AI Model** trained to recognize **player patterns**.
- **Variables** to track **player wins/losses**.

Code Snippet (AI Adapting Enemy Difficulty)

scratch

```
when green flag clicked
set player_wins = 0
set enemy_speed = 2

forever
   if (player_wins > 3) then
      increase enemy_speed
   else
      keep enemy_speed normal
```

- Now, the **enemy AI learns from the player's behavior and adapts dynamically!**

Using Speech Recognition for Interactive Games

Speech recognition allows players to **control games using their voice**, making gaming more immersive.

Example 2: Voice-Controlled Maze Game

Use case: A game where the player moves a character using voice commands like "Up," "Down," "Left," and "Right".

What You Need:

- **PictoBlox Speech Recognition Extension**
- **Sprite (Character) and Maze Background**

Step 1: Train AI for Voice Commands

1. Open **PictoBlox** → AI Extension → **Speech Recognition**.
2. Train the AI to detect **"Up," "Down," "Left," "Right"**.

Step 2: Control Game Character Using Voice

scratch

when AI detects "Up"
    move character up

when AI detects "Left"
    move character left

- Now, the **player can navigate the maze using voice commands!**

AI-Based Image Processing for Game Mechanics

AI-based image recognition allows games to **react to real-world objects**, such as **hand gestures or drawn shapes**.

Example 3: AI-Powered Drawing Game

Use case: A game where the player draws objects on paper, and the AI recognizes them to generate in-game effects.

What You Need :

- **PictoBlox Image Classifier**
- **Webcam for Real-Time Recognition**
- **Trained AI Model** to recognize **hand-drawn objects** (e.g., sun, tree, house).

Step 1: Train AI to Recognize Drawings

1. Open **PictoBlox** → AI Extension → **Image Classifier**.

2. Train the model to recognize **simple drawings like a sun, tree, and cloud**.

Step 2: Create Game Logic

scratch

when AI detects "Sun"
    change background to "Sunny Day"

when AI detects "Rain Cloud"
    start rain animation

- Now, players can **influence the game environment using real-world drawings!**

Hands-On Project: AI-Powered Rock-Paper-Scissors Game

Project Goal

- Players can play Rock-Paper-Scissors against an **AI** **opponent**.
- AI **recognizes the player's hand gesture** using a webcam.
- The game **automatically decides the winner**.

Step 1: Train AI to Recognize Hand Gestures

1. Open **PictoBlox** → **AI Extension** → **Pose Classifier**.
2. Train AI to recognize **three gestures**:
   - **Rock**
   - **Paper**
   - **Scissors**

Step 2: AI Decides the Winner

scratch

when AI detects "Rock"
    set player_choice = "Rock"

when AI detects "Paper"
    set player_choice = "Paper"

when AI detects "Scissors"
    set player_choice = "Scissors"

set AI_choice = pick random ["Rock", "Paper", "Scissors"]

if (player_choice = "Rock" and AI_choice = "Scissors") then
    display "You Win!"
else if (player_choice = AI_choice) then

```
    display "It's a Tie!"
else
    display "AI Wins!"
```

- The game **detects hand gestures and plays Rock-Paper-Scissors against the AI!**

Final Thoughts

In this chapter, you learned:
- How to create **AI-powered games** with adaptive enemies.
- How to implement **voice-controlled gaming**.
- How to use **AI-based image processing for interactive applications**.

Next, we'll explore **computer vision & AI-powered motion tracking**, where you'll build **gesture-controlled robots and smart security applications!**

Chapter 6: Real-World Applications and Case Studies

PictoBlox is not just a learning tool—it has real-world applications in **education, healthcare, smart cities, and industrial automation**. In this chapter, we will explore **how AI, robotics, and IoT using PictoBlox are transforming different industries**.

- **AI in Education** – Enhancing learning with interactive AI-based teaching.
- **Robotics in Healthcare** – Assistive robots for the elderly and disabled.
- **Smart Cities** – AI-powered traffic control and environmental monitoring.
- **Industrial Automation** – AI-driven efficiency in manufacturing.

AI in Education: Teaching with PictoBlox

AI is revolutionizing education by making learning **personalized, interactive, and engaging**.

Example: AI-Powered Virtual Tutor

Use case: A chatbot that helps students with math problems.

What You Need:

- **PictoBlox AI Chatbot Extension**
- **Pre-trained AI model for solving basic math problems**

Code Snippet (AI Tutor for Math Help)

scratch

```
when green flag clicked
ask "Enter a math problem:" and wait
set solution = AI solves math problem
say "The answer is: " + solution
```

- Now, the **AI tutor helps students solve math problems interactively!**

---

2 AI for Student Performance Analysis

AI can **analyze student performance** and give feedback based on their strengths and weaknesses.

Example: AI-Powered Quiz Analyzer

1. **Train an AI model** to recognize **correct and incorrect answers** from students.
2. **Use a confidence score** to provide **hints and suggestions**.

scratch

```
when student submits answer
   if (AI confidence score > 80%) then
      say "Correct! Great job!"
   else
      say "Try again! Here's a hint..."
```

- The **AI automatically provides feedback to students**!

Robotics in Healthcare and Assistive Tech

AI-powered robotics is **helping the elderly, assisting disabled individuals, and even performing surgeries**.

Example: AI-Based Assistive Robot for the Elderly

Use case: A robot that reminds elderly people to take medicine.

What You Need:

- **PictoBlox Speech Recognition & AI Chatbot**
- **Servo Motors (for robotic arm)**

Code Snippet (Voice-Activated Medication Reminder)

scratch

```
when AI detects "Did I take my medicine?"
    if (current time = medicine time) then
        say "Yes, you took your medicine."
    else
        say "No, it's time to take your medicine now."
```

- The **AI-powered robot reminds elderly users to take their medicine!**

2️⃣ AI-Powered Wheelchair Navigation

AI can help **autonomous wheelchairs navigate obstacles** using LiDAR and ultrasonic sensors.

Code Snippet (Obstacle Avoidance for Wheelchairs)

scratch

```
when green flag clicked
forever
    set distance = read LiDAR sensor
    if (distance < 20 cm) then
        stop motors
        turn right
```

- The **wheelchair detects obstacles and moves automatically!**

AI and IoT in Smart Cities

Smart cities use **AI and IoT** for **traffic control, environmental monitoring, and energy efficiency**.

Example: AI-Powered Traffic Management System

Use case: A smart traffic light that adjusts based on real-time vehicle flow.

What You Need:

- **Camera for vehicle detection**
- **PictoBlox AI Object Recognition**
- **IoT module for cloud data processing**

Code Snippet (Smart Traffic Light Control)

scratch

```
when AI detects "Heavy Traffic"
    extend green light time
else
    use normal traffic cycle
```

- The **AI automatically adjusts traffic light timings!**

2️⃣ Air Pollution Monitoring with AI & IoT

AI can **monitor air quality in real-time** and alert citizens when pollution levels are high.

What You Need:

- **MQ-135 Gas Sensor** (for air pollution detection)
- **ESP32 to send data to the cloud**

Code Snippet (AI-Based Air Quality Alert System)

scratch

```
when pollution level > threshold
    send alert "Air pollution levels are high! Wear a mask!"
```

- The **AI warns citizens about high pollution levels!**

Industrial Automation with PictoBlox

Industries use **AI and automation** to improve efficiency and reduce costs.

Example: AI-Powered Conveyor Belt Sorting

Use case: AI-based system that sorts objects on a conveyor belt based on color or shape.

What You Need:

- **PictoBlox Image Recognition**
- **Servo Motor for sorting mechanism**

Code Snippet (Sorting Items on a Conveyor Belt)

scratch

```
when AI detects "Red Object"
    move object to "Red Bin"

when AI detects "Blue Object"
    move object to "Blue Bin"
```

- The **AI automatically sorts objects based on their color**!

2️⃣ AI-Based Predictive Maintenance

AI can **detect machine failures before they happen**, reducing downtime.

What You Need:

- **Vibration Sensor for detecting machine faults**
- **AI model to analyze sensor data**

Code Snippet (Predicting Machine Failure)

scratch

```
when vibration level > normal range
    send alert "Machine needs maintenance!"
```

- The **AI warns technicians before a machine breaks down!**

Hands-On Project: AI-Powered Smart Parking System

Project Goal

- Detects **available parking spots** using AI and cameras.
- Sends **real-time parking availability updates** to a mobile app.

Step 1: Train AI to Detect Cars in Parking Spaces

1. Open **PictoBlox** → **AI Image Recognition**.
2. Train AI to recognize **empty vs occupied parking spots**.

Step 2: AI Detects Available Spots

scratch

when AI detects "Empty Spot"
   display "Parking Available"
else
   display "No Parking Available"

- The **AI-powered system guides drivers to available parking spots!**

Final Thoughts

In this chapter, you learned:
- How **AI in education** improves student learning.
- How **healthcare robotics** assist the elderly and disabled.
- How **AI and IoT** improve **smart cities and industrial automation**.

Chapter 7: Debugging and Performance Optimization

As your PictoBlox projects become more advanced, **debugging and optimizing performance** become crucial. AI models, robotics, and IoT projects require **efficient coding, optimized execution, and effective debugging strategies**.

In this chapter, you will learn:
- **How to train AI models efficiently** to reduce errors and improve accuracy.
- **How to optimize code for better performance**, especially in AI and robotics.
- **How to debug common issues** in complex projects.

Best Practices for Efficient AI Model Training

Training AI models properly ensures **higher accuracy, reduced bias, and faster predictions**.

Example: Optimizing an AI-Based Face Recognition Model

Use case: A facial recognition system for security that works with PictoBlox AI.

Common Mistakes in AI Training

- **Too Few Training Images** → Leads to **poor accuracy**.
- **Overfitting** → Model works on training data but fails on new data.
- **Unbalanced Dataset** → If 90% of images are of one person, the AI **struggles with new faces**.

Best Practices for AI Training in PictoBlox

+ **Use at least 100+ images per class**.
+ **Include diverse lighting conditions and angles**.
+ **Test with real-world data after training**.

Code Snippet (Validating AI Model Accuracy)

scratch

```
when AI model is trained
   if (accuracy > 85%) then
      say "Model is ready!"
   else
      say "Retrain with more images."
```

- Ensures the model **meets accuracy standards before deployment!**

Optimizing Code for Performance

Why is Optimization Important?

Poorly written code can lead to:
- **Slow execution times** in AI models and robotics.
- **Increased memory usage**, causing crashes.
- **Battery drain** in hardware-based projects.

Example: Optimizing a Smart Home IoT System

Use case: A PictoBlox project that **controls smart home devices over the internet.**

Problem: Slow Response Time

- The system **lags** when sending commands to the lights and fan.
- **Cause:** The code repeatedly sends API requests every second, overloading the system.

Solution: Use Event-Driven Optimization

- **Inefficient Code (Polling Every Second)**

scratch

```
forever
    send request to cloud server
```

+ **Optimized Code (Event-Triggered Requests)**

```
scratch
```

```
when button is pressed
    send request to cloud server
```

- Now, the system **only sends commands when needed, reducing lag!**

Example: Improving AI-Based Object Detection Performance

*Use case: A security camera that **detects people and alerts the owner.***

Problem: Frame Rate Drops When AI is Active

- The AI model **runs on every frame, slowing down video processing**.
- **Cause:** Running AI detection **too frequently**.

Solution: Process Every 5th Frame Instead of Every Frame

```
scratch
```

```
set frame_counter = 0

forever
    set frame_counter = frame_counter + 1
    if (frame_counter mod 5 = 0) then
        run AI detection
```

- Now, the AI **runs efficiently without slowing down the video feed!**

Debugging Common Issues in Advanced Projects

1□ Debugging AI Models in PictoBlox

Problem: AI Model Gives Incorrect Predictions

- **Possible   Causes:**
  - The dataset is too small.
  - The AI model is **not trained on diverse samples**.
  - The **background or lighting conditions** are different.

+   **Debugging   Steps:**
1□ Test the model with **different images**.
2□ Add more **training samples** with different lighting   and   angles.

3□ **Check AI confidence score** (if below 70%, retrain).

2□ Debugging Robotics and IoT Systems

Problem: Sensors Give Incorrect Readings

- **Possible   Causes:**
  - Faulty wiring or loose connections.
  - Sensor is **too close or too far** from the object.
  - Incorrect **threshold values** in the code.

+   **Debugging   Steps:**
Check sensor wiring with a multimeter.
Print **real-time sensor values** in PictoBlox to analyze   accuracy.
Adjust **threshold values** for better performance.

Example: Debugging an Ultrasonic Sensor in a Robot

scratch

```
when green flag clicked
    set distance = read ultrasonic sensor
    if (distance < 10 cm) then
        say "Obstacle too close!"
    else
```

move forward

- This code **verifies sensor readings before acting**!

3️⃣ Debugging Code Errors in Advanced Projects

Problem: The Project Crashes After Running for a While

- **Possible   Causes:**
  - Infinite loops consuming memory.
  - Too many sensor readings at once.
  - Overloaded AI processing.

+ **Debugging Steps:**

Use breakpoints to find infinite loops.
Print debug messages to track variable values.
Reduce AI model complexity for better performance.

Hands-On Project: Debugging a Smart Traffic Light System

Project Goal

- The system **adjusts traffic lights based on real-time car detection**.
- AI detects cars and **changes the light duration dynamically**.

Step 1: Identify the Bug in the Traffic Light System

scratch

when AI detects "Heavy Traffic"
    set green light duration = 10 seconds
else
    set green light duration = 5 seconds

Problem:

Traffic lights get stuck on green!

Cause:

-    The AI **keeps detecting cars** without a cooldown period.

Step 2: Fix the Bug with a Timer

+ Optimized Code with Cooldown Period

scratch

```
when AI detects "Heavy Traffic"
    if (time_since_last_change > 30 seconds) then
        set green light duration = 10 seconds
        set time_since_last_change = current time
```

- Now, the **AI adjusts traffic light duration efficiently**!

Final Thoughts

In this chapter, you learned:
- How to **train AI models efficiently** to reduce errors.
- How to **optimize code** for better performance.
- How to **debug robotics, AI, and IoT projects** with practical techniques.

Next, we'll explore **scaling AI and robotics projects**, where you'll learn **how to integrate PictoBlox projects with external APIs and cloud services!**

Chapter 8: Next Steps – Beyond PictoBlox

PictoBlox provides a great foundation for **AI, robotics, and IoT** using a visual programming approach. However, as you advance, you may want **more control, flexibility, and access to powerful AI frameworks**.

In this chapter, you will learn:
- How to **transition from PictoBlox to Python** for advanced AI development.
- How to **integrate PictoBlox with Raspberry Pi and Jetson Nano** for real-world applications.
- How to **explore open-source AI and robotics frameworks** to expand your knowledge.

Moving to Python and Advanced AI Tools

1️ Why Learn Python for AI and Robotics?

Python is the **most widely used language for AI, ML, and robotics**. Unlike PictoBlox's block-based coding, Python:
+ Allows **greater flexibility** in AI and robotics programming.
+ Supports **advanced AI libraries** like TensorFlow and OpenCV.

+ Enables **direct control over hardware** for robotics projects.

Example: Converting a PictoBlox AI Model to Python

*Use case: You built a **hand gesture recognition system** in PictoBlox, and now you want to upgrade it using Python.*

PictoBlox AI Model (Block-Based Approach)

scratch

when green flag clicked
    load AI model "HandGesture"
    forever
        if (AI detects "Thumbs Up") then
            say "Gesture recognized!"

Python Equivalent Using TensorFlow and OpenCV

python

import cv2
import tensorflow as tf

```
model                              =
tf.keras.models.load_model("hand_gesture_model
.h5")

cap = cv2.VideoCapture(0)

while True:
    ret, frame = cap.read()
    prediction = model.predict(frame)
    if prediction == "Thumbs Up":
        print("Gesture recognized!")
```

- **This Python version** gives full control over **model accuracy, frame processing, and AI performance**!

3□ Hands-On: Using Python to Control a Robot

Let's create a simple robot movement script using Python instead of PictoBlox.

PictoBlox Version (Block-Based)

scratch

```
when button "Move Forward" is clicked
    set motor speed to 100
    move forward
```

Python Version (Using Raspberry Pi & Motor Driver)

python

```python
import RPi.GPIO as GPIO
import time

motor_pin = 18
GPIO.setmode(GPIO.BCM)
GPIO.setup(motor_pin, GPIO.OUT)

def move_forward():
    GPIO.output(motor_pin, GPIO.HIGH)
    time.sleep(2)
    GPIO.output(motor_pin, GPIO.LOW)

move_forward()
```

- Now, your **robot can move using Python, unlocking more control and scalability**!

Combining PictoBlox with Raspberry Pi and Jetson Nano

1️ Why Use Raspberry Pi or Jetson Nano?

Both Raspberry Pi and Jetson Nano allow **faster AI processing and real-world applications** beyond PictoBlox's limitations.

Feature	Raspberry Pi	Jetson Nano
Best For	Robotics & IoT	AI & Deep Learning
CPU/GPU	Quad-Core CPU	Quad-Core CPU + GPU
AI Support	Basic AI (OpenCV, TensorFlow Lite)	Advanced AI (CUDA, TensorRT, Deep Learning)

Example: Integrating PictoBlox with Raspberry Pi

Use case: A smart security system that detects intruders using PictoBlox and Raspberry Pi.

Step 1: Use PictoBlox for AI Object Detection

- Train a **Face Detection Model** in PictoBlox.
- Export the trained model for use with Raspberry Pi.

Step 2: Use Raspberry Pi to Control Security Hardware

```python
python

import cv2
import tensorflow as tf
import RPi.GPIO as GPIO

model = tf.keras.models.load_model("face_detection_model.h5")
alarm_pin = 17

GPIO.setmode(GPIO.BCM)
GPIO.setup(alarm_pin, GPIO.OUT)

def detect_intruder():
    cap = cv2.VideoCapture(0)
    while True:
        ret, frame = cap.read()
        prediction = model.predict(frame)
        if prediction == "Unknown Face":
            GPIO.output(alarm_pin, GPIO.HIGH)
            print("Intruder detected!")
        else:
            GPIO.output(alarm_pin, GPIO.LOW)

detect_intruder()
```

- Now, the **security system can detect intruders and trigger an alarm** in real-time!

Example: Using Jetson Nano for Advanced AI

Use case: Real-time AI-powered object recognition for self-driving robots.

Why Jetson Nano?
+ It has **a built-in GPU for deep learning**.
+ Runs **YOLO (You Only Look Once) for object detection** in real-time.

python

```python
import cv2
import torch

model = torch.hub.load('ultralytics/yolov5', 'yolov5s')

cap = cv2.VideoCapture(0)

while True:
    ret, frame = cap.read()
    results = model(frame)
    results.show()
```

- Now, **your robot can detect and classify objects instantly!**

Exploring Open-Source AI and Robotics Frameworks

To move beyond PictoBlox, here are some powerful open-source frameworks:

Framework	Use Case	Best For
TensorFlow	Machine Learning	AI & Deep Learning
PyTorch	Deep Learning	Robotics & AI Research
OpenCV	Image Processing	Computer Vision
ROS (Robot Operating System)	Robot Control	Industrial Robotics
Arduino with Python	IoT & Automation	Hardware Control

Example: Using OpenCV for Object Tracking

Use case: A robot that follows an object using OpenCV.

python

```
import cv2

cap = cv2.VideoCapture(0)
tracker = cv2.TrackerMOSSE_create()
```

```
ret, frame = cap.read()
bbox = cv2.selectROI("Tracking", frame, False)
tracker.init(frame, bbox)

while True:
    ret, frame = cap.read()
    success, bbox = tracker.update(frame)
    if success:
        x, y, w, h = [int(v) for v in bbox]
        cv2.rectangle(frame, (x, y), (x+w, y+h), (255,
0, 0), 2)
    cv2.imshow("Tracking", frame)
```

- Now, **your robot can track and follow objects automatically!**

Final Thoughts and Next Steps

Congratulations! You've reached **the final chapter of this advanced PictoBlox guide**!

What You've Learned

+ **How to transition from PictoBlox to Python** for AI and robotics.
+ **How to use Raspberry Pi and Jetson Nano** for advanced applications.
+ **How to explore open-source AI and robotics frameworks** like TensorFlow, PyTorch, and ROS.

What's Next?

- **Experiment with Python and real-world AI projects.**
- **Build your own AI-powered robots with Raspberry Pi and Jetson Nano.**
- **Join open-source AI and robotics communities to keep learning.**

The world of AI and robotics is vast—keep exploring, keep innovating, and build the future

Disclaimer

"This book is an independent, unofficial guide to PictoBlox. It is not affiliated with, endorsed by, or sponsored by STEMpedia, the creators of PictoBlox. All trademarks, product names, and company names mentioned in this book belong to their respective owners. This guide is intended for educational purposes only, providing insights, tutorials, and hands-on projects to help users learn and explore PictoBlox effectively."

Table of Contents